Birdsongs and Twilight Hues

Jacob Oommen

ZORBA BOOKS

Published by Zorba Books, July 2024
Website: www.zorbabooks.com
Email: info@zorbabooks.com
Author Name: Jacob Oommen
Copyright ©: Jacob Oommen

Title: Birdsongs and Twilight Hues

Printbook ISBN: 978-93-5896-744-9
Ebook ISBN: 978-93-5896-081-5

The publisher under the guidance and direction of the author has published the contents in this book, and the publisher takes no responsibility for the contents, its accuracy, completeness, any inconsistencies, or the statements made. The contents of the book do not reflect the opinion of the publisher or the editor. The publisher and editor shall not be liable for any errors, omissions, or the reliability of the contents of the book.

Any perceived slight against any person/s, place or organization is purely unintentional.

Zorba Books Pvt. Ltd. (opc)
Sushant Arcade,
Next to Courtyard Marriot,
Sushant Lok 1, Gurgaon – 122009, India

Printed by Manipal Technologies Limited
A1 & A2 Shivalli Industrial Area Manipal Udupi, Karnataka – 57610

Dedication

For the dreamers, the wanderers, and the seekers.
For, this is your home.

Appreciation

Jacob Oommen is an incredibly gifted writer whose poetry never fails to inspire and delight. Through his masterful use of imagery and lyrical language, he so often captures the beauty of nature and the depth of human emotions. With verse that unfolds like a delicate melody, his work is a must-read for all poetry enthusiasts.

– **Bethany Samaddar** (@blsamadda),
Writer, USA

The enchantment of the seasons resides in Jacob Oommen's poems. He is one of the exemplary writers out there. It is simply humbling and an honour to read his words. His poems are like an artwork. I can simply visualise something out of a fairytale when I read his poems. He paints each line with his pen, creating a stunning landscape or a captivating imagery which I can picture vividly. His poems are truly magical and breathtaking.

– **Camellia** (@20_camellia),
Published Poet, USA

Jacob Oommen's poems are a daily joy to read. Written in many forms, they are always pleasant when read out loud. Full of vivid imagery, taking you across candid journeys of wonderment, escapisms, and down-to-earth realities. Explained beautifully, his poems capture the heart and give so much to reflect on.

They are full of charm and charisma, thoroughly recommended for peaceful evenings. They are indeed a great holiday read.

– **Fizzy Twizler** (@Fizzytwizler),
Published Author, London, UK

I love reading Jacob Oommen's wonderful poems. He writes from the heart, inspiring many. Everything is saturated with love and radiant warmth. His words seem to be sewn and painted with a silk brush. His wonderful poetic mind weaves the sublimity of poetry, and his phenomenal interest in strong spirituality inspires everyone.

– **Inna Orjola** (@IOrjola),
Writer, Crawley, England, UK

Jacob Oommen's creativity encompasses both the most immediate mundane state of being and the widest expanse of possibilities. His poetic vision and his role as a poet are to bring the work to those who need it. This is brilliantly crafted work by a talented writer.

– **Libbie** (@SoulScratches),
Writer and Author, Texas, USA

In an increasingly fragmented world full of chaos, we often crave serenity and tranquil silence. And Jacob Oommen's poetry provides such soothing comfort.

His poems are delightfully earthy and cosmic. Each poem explores the heights and depths of life and energy. His poems burst forth unhesitatingly from his pen, like a spontaneous exhale. His poems are not just literary devices strung together; they evoke unique vibrations by skilfully incorporating the enjambment of free verse. He takes us on a profound lyrical journey of romance, nature, and mysticism.

With masterful poetic acumen, Jacob has achieved metaphorical elegance and has given the world the gift of lyrical imagery to feel the senses, touch the heart and mind, and transfix the soul. He offers us a kaleidoscope of ubiquitous emotions, painting portrait after portrait of love, pain, and absolution. Jacob is a genius at weaving awe-inspiring images of ordinary moments and transforming them miraculously like the masterpieces of filigree art.

– **Monica B.** (@_Being_Benign),
Writer and Published Poet, India

Readers, prepare yourselves for sublime eloquence. *Birdsongs and Twilight Hues* will transport you to realms of wonderment and fascination. Each word is carefully chosen to craft poetry for the intellectual mind.

– **A.L. O'Prunty** (@OPruntyPoetess),
Poet, West Virginia, USA

Jacob Oommen's poetry delights all the senses with his beautifully descriptive language that extends beyond the everyday. His rich and expressive imagery, along with his unique poetic voice, is one that I've returned to re-read on many an occasion. *Birdsongs and Twilight Hues* contains the musicality and artistry of a poet in love with English language and nature, and I invite you to discover the magical world he creates.

– **C.X. Turner** (@lover__poetic),
Published Poet, Birmingham, UK

In Jacob Oommen's poetry, language becomes a sublime art. Verses come alive with sound, colours, and texture, immersing us in enchanting worlds where metaphors and imagery vividly play. Words simply carol in his mesmerising array.

– **Vanessa** (@poppies_me),
Poet, London, UK

Table of Contents

Acknowledgements

In the process of writing *Birdsongs and Twilight Hues*, I've realised the profound truth expressed in Psalm 127 of the Holy Bible: "Unless the Lord builds the house, the builders labour in vain." This has shown me how important it is to have God with us in everything we do. Without His guidance, this collection of poems would not have seen the light of the day. During my journey as a writer, I've felt His guiding hand shaping every word and every verse. I am grateful for His divine wisdom and grace that flow through these pages.

I am forever thankful for the support of my friends and followers on X (Twitter) since I joined the platform in 2021 and began sharing my poems. Their continuous encouragement has helped me become a better poet. In particular, I extend my deepest gratitude to Helen Laycock, the esteemed writer and Pushcart-nominated poet, who took the time to review the manuscript and provide invaluable suggestions. Additionally, I am thankful to Madhavi Sepuri Karri, a published poet, whose insightful feedback contributed to the polished quality of this book.

I express gratitude to Bethany Samaddar, Camellia, Fizzy Twizler, Inna Orjola, Libbie, A.L. O'Prunty, Monica B., C.X. Turner, and Vanessa for their appreciation of this book.

My mother always believed in me. Her support helped me much through my formative years. I am indebted to her for her constant encouragement, which gave purpose to my life.

Though she is no longer with us, her enduring love continues to inspire me every day.

Finally, to my caring, loving, and supportive family—my wife, Sabitha, and my daughter, Sarah—I extend my deepest gratitude. Your unwavering encouragement during challenging times has been a constant source of strength. Thank you for always standing with me and supporting me through thick and thin.

Preface

Words possess a magical quality capable of bringing calm and peace when used in the right way. They serve as a means for us to articulate our thoughts and emotions, conveying our innermost sentiments. It was during my academic journey that I developed a deep love for words. Inspired by the legends of English literature, I cultivated a passion for creating powerful verbal imagery through poetry.

In this book, I aim to convey feelings and sentiments engagingly, through vivid descriptions. My poems celebrate the beauty of nature, the nuances of human life, and the array of emotions, engaging the senses and emotions of my readers. I've crafted a lyrical melody, rhythm, and musicality in my poems.

For me, every poem is a miniature universe—complete, evocative, and meticulously crafted. Each word acts as a brushstroke, inviting readers to the world of my imagination, where every petal, every gust of wind, and every heartbeat tells a story.

Within these pages, you will find contemporary free verse poems inviting the reader to sway to the rhythm of my inspiration. Each poem serves as an expression of the themes that bind this collection.

I'm excited to share this book with you, as each poem holds significant meaning for me. I hope they resonate with you, bringing moments of reflection, inspiration, and joy.

Foreword

Whenever I read Jacob Oommen's work, it strikes me that he doesn't just write, but rather *paints* poetry. His palette of description is unparallelled as he selects the most exquisite tapestry of colour, embellishing it with light effect and sound, to create scintillating wordscapes which frame nature at its best.

How delicately Jacob captures the holly blue butterfly in *Cadenced Sways*, for example:

Lit by the liquid dawnlight,
she swings to the crystal rustles
of a dulcet wind chant,

and how beautifully portrayed is the *Albino Hummingbird*:

Clad in
twilight shadows
of silver calligraphy,

Magic is created over and over in this collection, here through sibilance in *April's Tender Tryst*:

Sylphic grail of a night blooming jasmine—

in sterling swells of silksong weaves,
soft swirls of a floral scent effuse
in arias of honey and saffron,

A wonderful surprise, too, was how the visual focus changes to one of physicality as we are treated to *bouncy wingbeats, boisterous swings* and *nimble backflips* in the poem, *Mischievous Wind.*

These poems sing and delight, each phrase an observational gem. It has been a pleasure and an honour to be the first to savour *Birdsongs and Twilight Hues.*

– Helen Laycock,
Writer, Pushcart-nominated poet, UK

Helen Laycock is a Pushcart-nominated poet, recipient of the David St. John Thomas Award, nominee for the Dai Fry Award and recent winner of Black Bough Poetry's Chapbook contest. Her collection *Frame* has featured as Book of the Month at the East Ridge Review.

Her writing has appeared at *Reflex Fiction,* the *Ekphrastic Review,* the *Cabinet of Heed, Visual Verse, Onslaught Press, Folkheart Press, Prattlefog and Gravelrap, The Wombwell Rainbow, Poetry Roundabout, Spilling Cocoa Over Martin Amis, Paragraph Planet, Serious Flash Fiction, Flash Flood, The Best of CafeLit, The Beach Hut, Popshot, Lucent Dreaming, Full Moon and Foxglove, The Caterpillar, The Dirigible Balloon, Literary Revelations, Black Bough, The Storms Journal, Broken Spine Arts, Fevers of the Mind,* et al.

LEAVES OF FIRE

Swirling dapples, chattering potpourri,

tangled in an orchestral palette,
a riot of russets, scarlets and lustrous saffron.

An irised huescape
awash in ethereal aura.

Autumn leaves—

they flutter on the nymphic wingbeats
of October zephyr,

waltzing to the lilts of its carolling caress.

A melange of rustles, earthy copper
and burnt cinnamon,

their nacreous luminance shimmer
in ripples of amber and iridescent green.

Soft, swishing swings of oriflamme yearning
in tourmaline's vibrant symphony.

WILD BLUEBELLS

Beneath the brushstrokes
of emeralds and ancient oak,

draped in hues of azure haze,

chimes of cobalt marble
whirl in a wispy tapestry of florid aquarelle.

Sapphirine streaks
of chiffon and cashmere.

Bathed in gentle light,
scattered winks of neon buds undulate
in a cradling serenade of jewel-like rhythm.

Velveteen hums of bees,
beryl butterflies, periwinkle spell,

whispering oracles of a sirenic charm—

wild bluebells,
spring's rhymesters of a verdant rhapsody.

WINGS OF SHIFTING COLOURS

Feral frenzy of a rainstorm—

damned, disillusioned,
a damselfly flew to the petal lap
of the lorn, forlorn sky,

where, in grosgrain whorls of glossy burnish,
the sun mixed mystic zaffre mist
in ritzy shimmer,

blew the blush, flushing bliss
on her luminescent wings.

Behold!
In beats of delicate alchemy,

the damselfly morphs into
woven strands of stained glass, jade and celadon.

Lyrical breaths
in latticed glister of gossamer wreaths,

she becomes the iridescence
of a timeless ballad.

TWINKLER NIGHT

Cadenced swells of luminous sequins,
glo-pearl sways of sprinkled ember.

Lacquered moondust,
the night sky shines in frosty twinks of opal blobs.

Ochre and frescos on dusk's basalt brocade—

fireflies in filigree flare,
like a thousand fairy lights' flicker.

In welkin's spangled splendour,

they weave kindled contrails
in synchronal twinkling,

and like edelweiss and spiky stapelia,
bloom in heavens' floral meadows.

PETAL-WET ANEMONES

Raindrops—

tethered to the cirrus tendrils,

confetti of silver crystals
that enthral the parched earth
in hypnotic petrichor.

Amongst the harebells
and bronze-leafed heucheras,

anemone blooms
wave in melodies of liquid plops and carnelian.

Afroth, they marvel in brushstrokes
of lucent acrylic

to the drumming staccatos
that scribble lauds
in garnets and gilt-edged rainbows.

In celestial splendour,

shrivelled dreams revive in cosy embrace
of a summer's refreshing shower.

SPRING'S SECOND COMING

Honeyed gold, merlot and magenta,
jewelled radiance of fiery berry-reds.

Ferns and aspens,
maples and clouds' calico contours,
ceaseless rustles of a sizzling blaze.

Autumn, it's spring's second coming.

Kindred souls of teasels and fuchsia
tangled in sheeny candescence.

In swirling colours
of sunstones and vermilion,

they soak my senses,

dapple my sky in runic rings
of quartz and clavinet,

drape my cravings in muralled braids
of corals and clematis.

WISTFUL... IT'S WISTERIA

In the barrens of frost and bony trees,
arrays of sprightly dryads,

lacy halos of azures and amethyst.

Zesty wisteria,

cascades of coruscant plumes
trailing like tinsels of festooned daylight

as they sway in the morning shadows
of a bubbly blue breeze, entwined.

In hued iridescence of idyllic lilts,

they sing music of white musk and lilac
in gaita notes of raw silk and spectral warbles.

FLAMINGOS IN FLIGHT

Across the withered vermeils
of the winter-worn sky,

rosy pink,
elegance of a slick, glossy dazzle.

Mystic sweeps of sunset topaz,
orris and flamboyance.

A palette of fluorescent beryls, luscious scarlets
glimmer in charmeuse trim—

lo, blooms of flamingos in flaming symphony.

At the horizon,
like echoes of a rustic folk song,
they fade in the lulling veils of a violescent skyline.

A GARDEN FOR A FLOWER

Mesmerised by the paeans
of your earthy mustards, iris and zinnias,

O spring!

I asked for a single flower—
a keepsake of your spellbinding mystique.

But you gave swells of bliss,
psalms and songbirds
in bouquets of vernal glyphs.

In angelic ecstasy,

every bough bursts with citreous mirth,
pansy purples and aureolin ruffle.

Woodsy scent of oud and sandalwood,

a sacred shade of charm
drifts in frilly carnations of flitting butterflies,

while, twilight blazes in April's agate reds.

MOONLIT MUSINGS

Beneath the shroud of onyx,

graphite midnight of katydids
and emerald summers,

wafts of fleecy ivory
curl up in milky opalescence of velvet weaves.

Full moon—
ballads of lyrical light's perpetual longing.

Like whispering sprites
in broadsweeps of alabaster spell,

she croons an etheric serenade
in amber and splendour of scribbled silver.

Downy drizzles of pearls and mysteries,

heavens' bloodstone revelations in spectral accents
as she shimmers in syllables of a lucent lullaby.

GOLDEN FLAMENCO

Ethereal resonance
of the eloquent hang drum,

it kindles her sleek silhouette
to a fiery ember in timeless tales
of cerulean infinity.

In gossamer spells of rusty copper
and cantaloupe

she swings to the fairy chimes
of a sibylline plainchant in soulful duende.

Like windblown leaves of hazels,
rubies and goldenrod,

she soars in graceful leaps and twirls
of autumn's artful sonnet.

EXCITED ROBIN

Weathered shards,
nacreous rhyme, sunshower chorales
of liquid jewels.

In the misty taffeta of bluish shadows,
forest songs and lazy bodhran refrains

sits a robin redbreast bleeding petalled lilts.

Kvelled, heart awhirl,
she calls out to me in a dreamy soliloquy

to watch a crimson sunbeam
slice a raindrop

unleashing a dayglo rainbow's
tendrilled heartbeats.

Elysian poesy,
graffiti of a dappled melody,

unfurling muse of surreal magick.

SPRING RAIN

Forlorn earth
shrouded in creeping greys of dreary grief.

A rimy land
drowned in winter woes
of wasted clouds and ceaseless requiems.

Betwixt the sombre thrums
of noir and threnody,

echoes of cup chimes and tambourines unfold—
rainsongs in chrome's lustrous aura.

In lulling ripples of laughs and carols,
breaths of lime and fragrant mint,

zen-like whiffs of wispy petrichor rise
to caress the ghastly pall of the bluesy chaos.

Behold,
in neon notes of coral and vermilion,

the parched earth wakens
in wren's spring songs of aureolin,

blushes in hues of chirrs and chirrups,
crocus and clover blooms.

CHAFFINCH'S LOST SPRING SONG

Blazing tangerines,
flaming sunsongs in florid flourish,

cherry blossoms in fiery emberglow.

Woodland birds,
buzzing bumblebees,
scarlet splashes in beaming brilliance,

lullabies of a springtime dawn.

Perched amidst the orchid buds,
a lone chaffinch—

atrous sigh of a wintry lament.

Unsung, she mourns her frayed,
frazzled heartstrings,

thirsts for ancient lores
and curls of rhythmic euphonies

to unravel spring hymns
in the weary throbs of her midnight soul.

TULIPS' TIMELESS WALTZ

Aubergine sheen,
crystal flares in peppy, rippling syllables.

They unfurl as ethereal warbles
of a charmed love song—

ballads of tulips
in purple opulence
in orchard's blissful harmony.

Flirty faes,
May's hums of a windy harp
cartouched in velvet whispers of amethyst chorus.

They sway to the cradling croons
of a balletic breeze in honeyed cadence.

IN ZIGS AND IN ZAGS

From the darkened contours
of a bloated thundercloud,

burnished in chartreuse trim,

bolts of lightning dart in sizzling dazzles
of a blinding flash.

Like dancing strands of rose and gold,

in dizzying zigs and saffron zags,
they zip down the horizon
in fleeting streaks of lanky lucency,

and paint choric scores in alluring murals
of flaxen flair.

With arias of sparkling swirls,
they serenade the sea, seagulls and pebble jades
to a gilded shade of oneiric shimmer.

CHICK-A-DEE MELODIES

Twilight fractals of a frenzied ditty,
chirruping contrails of a streaming symphony—

perched on a red maple,
quilled and crested, a black-capped chickadee.

Her visceral chirps
waft like drifting whiffs of aloeswood incense,

linger in the threaded agate braids
of lilac and lavender skies.

In the woodwind chords of cedars and old oaks,

the draped spring morn
breaks into pirouettes of an auburn rune
in hazel accents of the radiant birdsong.

SIGHS OF A WITHERED FLOWER

The last petal fallen,
waning mana of crimson charm.

In the arid cold of the forgotten corner,
a gloomy flower moans her
evanished splendour.

Ruined and ravaged,
her ribcage whines in bluesy woes.

Wistful,

she craves for the
emerald sprinkling of earth's riddles
snugged in her moonstone womb

to primp spring's spinel palette
with tincts of daffodils, ruddy cardinals

and hasten the aching hungerings
of the winter-wrecked woodland.

SONGLESS BLACKBIRD

In the chasmic voids of the alien skyline,
'midst ravens and louring greys,

doleful knells of fading woodsmoke.

The howling wind, its grievous cry,
whispers of haunting scores,

sobs of a monotone dawn.

Weary, in winter's darkest hour
as gelid filigrees weave their hoary chill,

a red-winged blackbird aches for her lost chorus.

In wordless trills and scattered wingbeats,

like tangled cello strings that whine
strains of an elegiac monody,

she wails for oblivion.

SUMMER SUNSET

In speckled rustle, sequined flutter,
amidst the flaring damask,

upon the porcelain lustre of a dreamy albatross,

mermaids and sea nymphs
soar in billows of gilt and shadows

fading into the latticed echoes
of dusk's warm-toned bloodstone.

They paint the setting sun in blazing gouache
of bespoke brushstrokes.

Lo, the rust and eventide
shimmer in coloured streaks of a celestial arioso—

like iridescent drops of peony reds and astral purples.

DRIED AND DROOPED

In endless emptiness,

bronzed embers fade into
cinereous wisps of orphaned hues.

Frail and forlorn,
the rugosa grieves her crêpe pink poesy.

Clad in pallid shrouds
of black mist and barren clouds,

she chants her laments and litanies
in muted rhymes.

Her trailing sighs,
like requiems of ash and shattered halos,

surge in crescendos of a desolate dream's
sable mourns.

Stripped of her rubellite glory,
in the aches and agony of a sombre windsong,

deadened, she droops.

YELLOW WARBLER

In the land of the raspberry springtide,

amidst the soft psalms
of cherries and ethereal fairies,

rufescent bursts,
rouge and ruby in lyrical refrains—

first call of the unveiling dawnglow.

Merry mirth, chattering cheeps,
swells of an irised chorus uncurl—

a warbler, in sunlit gold.

She flies to the sylvans
of the peach-tinged skyscape

and becomes the silver syllables
of the auburn mornlight.

She blazes
as its russet dazzles
kindle her quilled longings to a rustling blush

in shades of a nuptial serenade.

WATERFALL, MELODY FLOWS

Down the weathered cliff,
through the moss green rocks,

chants of fizz, cascades of sudsy gems.

Waterfall.

Mellifluous,
its lucent folds of tinsels and brilliance
sing in bubbly merriment.

Lacy ripples
in lush avalanches of white pearls
and powdered zircon

as it plummets in beryl glides
of chrome and marble spray.

In soaring susurrus of babbling baubles,
it foams and burbles an anthem
of fluid incantation.

In never-ending crystals and abstracts,
hums of ancient lullabies unfold.

SEA SYMPHONY

Music of the Seven Seas—

like augural oracles
that bloom in the cornet symphonies
of petals and milky pebbles,

they trance in the chasmal depths
of the sea's troubadour soul
amidst swirls of ebony silk and liquid ripples.

On full moon nights,
when the sea wakens to the whispers
of cosmic songs,

in endless refrains,

they unfurl as silent echoes
of mermaids' sonata strums

in the frosted tangerines
of queen conch shells.

SNAPSHOTS OF A SHOOTING STAR

Hazel jewels that bask in the womb
of a rubied mystery,

astral verses of darting glitter
that waltz through the moonlit cobalt

strewing ornate drizzles of diamond dust—

shooting stars.

Pearlescent flares
that carve chandelier-like glints,

they weave argyle tapestry of carmines
and garnet strands.

Fleeting dreams,
nestled on the sizzling wings of thunderbirds,

they glide across the velvet purple of the night skies
scattering sprinkles of topaz and firelight.

SAFFRON SEA DANCE

Ashen waves crash in aching breaks.

At the shoreline,
they wail wild, roaring in mournful blue,

like an antsy sea nymph frothing out
her soul's arcane grief.

But, on that dark, dismal dusk,
the sun mixed fiery crimson

in amorous strokes of love-laced roseate
to soothe her distraught waves.

As I watched,
jovial waves surged in rhythmic swells
of lacy gold and silky saffron.

FIREFLY SPARKLERS

Fireflies at the skysill.

Twinkles of burnt beryl,
winking flames of amber and emerald.

They weave gossamer murals
with vibrant swirls of mystic light.

On the tendrils of oneiric ripples,

they whorl up in spells of cadenced flair
to the obsidian abyss of the ageless sky,

like clouds of sinuous whispers.

In filigree flourish,
primal odes of fluorescent opals flare out,

like sparkling fireworks of jewelled iridescence.

NIGHTINGALE CALLS

Amongst the lyrical lilts of tourmaline warbles,
sonorous rapture of a sweet,
silvery soprano.

Spirited bursts of sirenic chirrups—

a nightingale's choral symphony.

In cerise embrace,
they wrap me, caress me, rekindling amethyst echoes
of windy whistle tweets.

Windswept choons of winter pipers,
rubescent haze of an entrancing mystery.

Like folk songs that cruise on rustic winds,

serene, soft-floating notes of a
two-note cradle song.

GLOWING SEEDLING

In the burnt umber
of the scorched earth, zizzed a tiny seed.

It longed for the sizzling kiss of the spring
to unfurl life in her gravid womb.

Skyward she gazed.

In frenzy,
a fiery raindrop in pearly berceuse

riding on earth scents of moss
and meadowlarks, soared down to cheer her.

Behold,

the flushed blush of the gleaming seedling

as it springs forth in anthems of
cedar-scented geraniums.

SUMMER OF FIREFLIES

Beaming in the midnight's moondust verse,

swarms of sparkly amber
in ember's malachite glister,

wings of light,
fractals of burnished baubles—

a web of twinkling fireflies.

Donned in finespun flashes of chartreuse flare,
like forest sprites that scribble rhymes
of a nighttime chorus,

they scrawl fables in throbs of curlicues
in jades and furbished wheat

as they fly and flicker in sleek opal winks.

AUTUMN RAINBOW

On the wet western sky
where cobalt and shadows float,

tendrils of opalescent glaze.

In brushstrokes of painted radiance,
soft tints diffuse in autumn's dappled palette.

From crimsons to violets, a coloured rainbow
dreams.

While, across the scattered silhouettes
of the vespertine's dusklight,

in pumpkin pink and roseate lustre,
medleys of gilded runes twirl.

In glistening sapphire,
carols of dazzling cloudlight ablaze.

LIGHT, ITS SHADE

Pewter clouds in graphite weaves
surging like taupe-toned candy floss.

Rainstorm blossoms in monochrome streaks
flowing like carrara marble moiré drapes.

They climb the azure of the endless sky
and draw lustrous charcoal contours

of green-eyed rain nymphs
rollicking to the drumroll staccatos
of rumbling thunder

in lacy filigrees of toneless lead.

In tequila sweeps,
sun's golden rays carve bronze wizardry
across the dove greys of the heavens

in motifs of aery chiaroscuro—

a rare brilliance in strands of wispy graffiti.

EVER-CHANGING OCEANSCAPE

You baffle me with your many moods—

woeful moan, calming melody,
blustery temper, quirky upsurge.

In dawns and in sunsets,
you sing lullabies to the sky and the boundless horizon.

In the day's mauveine hues,
you swim in turquoise,

in fluid euphony of seagulls and sea glass swirls.

With the night's raven calls,
your depths echo tales of ancient myths
and forgotten chronicles.

Haunting mysteries slumber in you.

In stillness you trance
in the abyss of your being,

curls into blue blurbs of solitude.

But, when your waters whirl in feral wrath,
mercurial cadence,

I'm confused, O unfathomable ocean!

SPIDER'S WINTER ART

A spider on its silken loom
on a flaming forsythia's gnarling limb.

Charming agate of an opal psalm,

it glimmers in hyaline glow,
awakens to the hums of a primal hymn.

Rippling in twilight's lulls and rhythms,

it weaves labyrinths of ornate glister
in milky sheen.

Like a beryl bloom,

it shimmers as it sways

on the misty wings of a cabriole breeze.

Entranced, a drizzly drop of a dreamlike dew
rests upon the gossamer web.

Wreathed amulet,
an iridescent tessera that swings
in morn's whites and wintry splendour.

FOREST'S ALLURE

An enchantress,

you lure me into the alluring tangles
of your rapturous bliss,

where linnets and blackcaps
chirrup in cherry-red arias,

where rustling chorales
ramble on the whims of a sportive draught,

where shrunken streams
bask in their white pebbly delights.

In your viridian merriment,
time fades in whistle-wind whispers
of birdsongs and emerald musings.

O woodland!

To say farewell, my soul aches.

I leave a beat of my heart
to amble with your roving breath
perennially in your winsome soulscape.

METEOR MARVEL

Blazing tassels, sparkly fractals,
jewelled firelight flames in fiery flourish.

Like emberwings,
they flash on flickering diamond flecks,

bleed azuline flute notes
of nighttime chanson in amberina.

Leonid shower—

fireball flurry,
fleeting scatter of auburns in starburst trim.

They soar in revelry,
blazing across the dewy dark,

carving surreal allegories
of lilies and lightwashed gems,

unfurling a ritzy tapestry of spellbinding glitz.

BRIDAL DANCE

Autumn zephyr,

a wandering bard
on whistling whorls of silver.

He sails through sunlit susurrus,

whizzing, weaving wispy rhapsodies
in chords of fairy folklore.

Amorous caress,

a casuarina breaks into a bridal serenade,
her sprite-like crest aglow in emerald lilts.

Svelte and sinuous,
she sways in ceaseless ripples,

like a danseuse's sprightly twirls.

Swooshing symphony,
silken swirls of ochre runes,
dulcet cadence of a windchime melody.

BUBBLE MAGIC

Tethered to the sibilance
of a wester whisperwind,
nacreous orbs of sylphlike dryads.

Draped in lacy kirtles of drifting glitter,
like windblown rainbows, webs of dandelions,
they ascend in a wingless glide.

Soap bubbles,

lustrous blobs of a mesmeric riff
in pearlescent hues.

In the boundless tangerines of the sunshine
they dissolve,

glistening as they wane,
leaving golden flecks of glowing aureoles

in honeyed effervescence
of bubbly mirth.

NOMAD OF THE LONELY SKIES

In solitary flaps of cobalt wings,
you whoosh through the wintry greige
of the antique sky,

like swirls of zircons and meteorites
spilling mazarine drizzles in dazzling fluorescence.

As you sweep through the cloudscape,

primal spells of your roving soul
swing to the mantic descants

of celestial faes that lullaby you
on your sibylline path.

Blue heron—

a nomad on timeless quest for mystic shores
in silent wafts of fading shadows.

GLORIOUS, EVERY MORNING

Vagrant curls of milky mist
in radiant weaves of ethereal filigree.

It trickles through the
lush, leafy canopy of the rolling vale

stirring wild grass
and tender buds of winter flowers
snug in its sheeny comfort.

Morning Glory—

dawn's own charmed daughter
born of dew and windswept meadows,

damsel in the luminous veil of December's solitude.

She blooms
in pristine gloss of rhymes and amethyst

to the frost-kissed allure of purple nymphs
in timeless rituals of ephemeral blush.

Amidst the petalled dazzle,
radiance of the winter sun swells.

CADENCED SWAYS

On the stray tendril of a woodland ivy,
a holly blue butterfly.

Lit by the liquid dawnlight,
she swings to the crystal rustles
of a dulcet wind chant,

like blinks of sapphire bubbles
in azure's dappled translucence.

Autumn's whispered descants
of mauve and damask rose
unfold in her legato lilts

as she sways in silky ripples
of a willowy danseuse.

BALLET IN THE SKY

In garnet sparkle,
a kite rassles with the frenzy of the zephyr,

climbs the delft porcelain of the skyscape
to evanesce in the sun's gentle embrace.

Cradled by the
aureate rays' braided opulence,
she sails,

swirls with brushmarks
of flailing streamers
in jasper and cherry-red radiance.

Her harlequin splendour
twirls like a sequined ballerina.

Graceful glissades,

she revels in the chrome and petals
of the summer's sunstone sheen.

ORIOLE CHORUS

Perched on a mulberry branch,

crimson orioles,
alluring carollers of the dawn canzonet.

In choral chirrups,
a zingy rhapsody they sing,

their sonorous trills
resound amidst spring's mystic tongues
of rubied calls.

Their festal odes—
rufescent refrains of April's bubbly delight
in cheery strains.

They wrap the winter-warped wasteland
with chintz and chenille of tourmaline,

like rich viol spells of vernal gaiety.

MISCHIEVOUS WIND

In fluid glides of bouncy wingbeats,

a brisky wind soughs through the grasslands
in glyphic waves of festive mirth.

With frenzied passion,
he whizzes through the treetops
in boisterous swings,

whirls them to his whims, his verdant yearnings.

In nimble backflips, he tousles the boughs,
swishes them in sibilant sways of silken barcaroles.

Loose-limbed sweeps,

through the grove and the sylvan gorge,
spry, spirited serenade of his crazy pranks.

ODE TO A CUCKOO

In the rustle of leaves
hides a melody, soulful as a lonely call.

Sweet stirring paeans
only fairy nymphs can sing,

angelic hymns of an emerald cuckoo.

In the woods,
high in the canopy she dwells,

a riddle
wrapped in a haunting mystery.

In tones of
bloodstones and clarinet,

she leaves echoes of a resonant whistle

as she flies away into the tangles of the piney copse.

A tiny song,
fleeting chorus, fade-out notes
in twilight's paling flame.

JEWEL OF THE NIGHT SKY

On the lucent lowlight of the zaffre sky,

in filigree shimmer,
auburn cords that weave orphic psalms
of light and starlit serenade.

Flary Sirius,
jewel of the midsummer night
as it sentinels the moonstone of the antique skies.

A gold griffin
that graces the ritzy frieze of the darklit sky,

its citrine embers light up
like trails of faes and wispy fireflies.

Through timeless chronicles,
it chants charms to the cold silhouettes
of the solitary earth

in sparkles of dazzles and fire streaks.

APRIL'S TENDER TRYST

Sylphic grail of a night blooming jasmine—

in sterling swells of silksong weaves,
soft swirls of a floral scent effuse
in arias of honey and saffron,

ascending the sable satin of the moonlit sky
in dainty tendrils.

Rubious euphoria,
ardent wisps of ecstasy.

Bewitched,
a hawkmoth, draped in copper's lustrous veil

croons a feisty solo of tender romanza
in harp notes of rose quartz
in April's marvel and vermilion.

In spring's accents of primrose and moonflower,

they sway to the choons of amour
and luminous starlight.

ALBINO HUMMINGBIRD

Clad in
twilight shadows
of silver calligraphy,

like whispering specks
of relucent clouds in albescent glister,

a hummingbird wafts down,

perches on the petalous green
of a cypress shoot.

She broods in pensive stillness of onyx white,

like tiny tufts of fluffy snow
that braids strands of silent echoes.

Rhythm of a cryptic mystery awakens
in scribbles of scarlet ferns and flowered trilliums.

MOONLIT HOWL

Low-slung on the silken cobalt
of the brumal sky,

milky luminance that casts
spellbinding radiance—

amber and opalescence
of the winsome full moon.

Awash in vestal glaze of ageless alabaster,
she glows like a danseuse's lilting lustre.

Down the vale,
in midnight's ebon, obsidian maze,
a glum-blue wolf—

silhouette of grieving grey.

Swathed in cinereous haze,
lone and forlorn, he yowls a mournful dirge—

woeful wails of leaden grief.

Rippling refrain,
nocturnes of the wolf's aurulent longing

for the far-flung moon.

OCEAN'S FLAMING PINK

Lullabied by the lacquered sun,

like an elusive flash,
a flamingo flits through the azurescape
of the mid-heavens.

'Neath, on the scintillant jewels
of the turquoise ocean

floats a mystery in erubescent rouge—

her irised shadow,
like a mirage of coral sigils.

A charmed amulet
in gold and pink's flamboyance,

she soars, gliding and floating,
like hums of a soulful sonata,

and wanes in the eventide
of the sky's molten melodies.

PURR-SUITS

Ivory dazzle, stippled sparkle,

zesty bursts of frolic
in agate's sapphirine eyes.

Mews and pearlescence in canorous sways.

Bouncy, she slinks in sleeky swings,
sassy, she springs in prankish fizz.

In languid yawns,
she slithers in stealthy silence

curling up in arabesque swirls.

A puddle of woolly fur
in fluffy, fleece ball weaves.

Brindled contours of a dappled rag doll—
a cutie cuddly kitty cat.

PROMISE OF A NEW DAWN

In shades of white jade
with lustrous streaks of gold and honeydew,

gentle embrace of a nebulous glow.

Sequined shivelight—

it braids sunlit shards of astral strobes
through the glossy green of the barked birches.

On firebird's wingbeats of blazing twilight,
cascades of malachite and cutglass,

verses of a choral paean unveil.

Whiffs of tuberose and apricots
'midst the rhythmic throbs of a rustic canticle.

In the accents of an orphic presong,
the lavender of a new dawn unfurls.

Joy swells, my spirit soars.

HOPES AND BLOOMS

Bluesy blurbs of a gloomy winter,
its creeping grips of ghostly greys
and grizzled cobwebs.

'Neath the waning wisps of silver
and woodsmoke,

shrivelled shadows of lazy mist
wilt.

In the numbed emptiness,

I hibernate.

I wait

for the spring's tender knock
on the frozen shell of my tangled longings,

for it to rouse the dormant blush
of my rainbow's jewelled chroma—

like a ruddy flush spritzing glittery fractal.

And play vibrant melodies
of freesias and tinted hyacinths
on my splintered heartstrings.

DESIRE TO FADE OFF

Silhouettes
break into aching chaos,

veiled in the ashen shrouds
of an evanescent swansong,
cries of dying colours.

Empty beats,
haunting refrains
of banshees and abaddon black.

Witch hour caws,
raven cries of dark's griseous silence.

Ebony blooms,
cloud flowers of a stormy evenfall.

In sighs, hazy hues,
paling ruins of a broken skyline

bleeds.

Buried in shades of
noir, onyx and oboe notes,

claw marks of a withered ember—

my yearning for oblivion.

LOST CHILDHOOD

Summer rain,
staccato thrums of cadenced incantation.

Saudade,
chants of dewy-eyed sepia.

In its midst,

the fairy maiden grieves her lost childhood
of wet scents and drizzle-kissed thistles,
chrysanthemums.

Mourns the rosy spells she cherished—

chasing the bonny blue butterflies,

dancing to the frenzied timpani
of a rustic downpour,

tailing the liquid psalmody
of cuckoo's woodland symphony,

vanishing in the origami rhymes
of ethereal petrichor.

FIRE BAPTISM

A fiery lightning
in flips of tangerine flourish, sparkling brilliance.

Like crystal shards of red spinel,

it dives into the frozen fathoms of the ocean
to its delusions,

baptises it with scarlet flares
of its diamond flames.

Euphoric,
at the shore, in curling breaths
of fizz and crested mirth,

its tabernacle waves sacralise me,
carries me to the depths of its ineffables,
its mystery,

stirs my scattered hankerings
in the burnt frankincense of its sacred fire.

Behold, like the fabled phoenix,

I rise from the chimaeras of a surreal dreamscape.

VOYAGE

A muddy river
wades through the vacuous chasms
of boundless chaos in flustered ripples

amidst murky echoes of endless elegies

to dump its guilt in the ocean
for a clear conscience.

In timeless arias of surging sapphires,
bubbling laughter,

the ocean receives,

cleanses,

sets her free.

As I watched,
in bliss and in bubbles,
the river soars towards the horizon

in silver bursts of a coral sonata
on the croceate trails of a rapturous wave.

MEETING THE REAL SELF

Lustral chorales and amber chronicles—

like delphic psalms,
they travel on bracing mistral winds.

Seven Seas
converge in the stillness of an arcane heart
in crystals and in purity.

Sky empties its azure yearnings
in the wispy turquoise of the abyssal depths

where the seas first filled their sacred music
in the whorls of the conch shells.

A gilded cauldron of halcyon mystery.

There, in the ethereals
of twilight's purple haze, myriad pastels,

you met your real self—

a mystic in blood-red radiance.

NOSTALGIA

Dawn wakens in dewy neon,

cherries and daffodils sway in
honeyed opulence.

Woodlarks,
sibilant grove's bronzed choristers
hum their emerald mornsong.

Runic thrums of autumn's auburn rain rhymes.

Arid earth, tinder dry,
now dazed, drunk on petrichor.

In the quiet of the October rainstorm,
whispers of forgotten dreams return.

Amidst the hues of woodsmoke and sepia,
I mourn the copper notes of a stolen bliss.

Aching waves of echoes swell,
like haunting peals of a cracked carillon.

BALLADEERS

Thin thoughts turn breezy spectres,
cruise the cosmic void,

unfurl life in rubescent carols.

They weave through the warp of my dreams,
a weft of tendrilled lingering

creating my reality.

They flood the parched songbirds
with canorous riffs,

tinge the shrivelled rainbows
with blushing colours,

crimson the setting sun
with svelte strokes of crystal fire.

My thoughts are balladeers—

wandering troubadours of wordless lullabies
awakening solitary souls.

A HYMN TO SPRING

Fiery ire of the feral lightning,

roaring wrath of the raucous thunder,

swirling fury of the squally tempest.

Myth hour groans,
haunting echoes of nightjar's ghostly calls.

Fated trysts,
your life scripts in glyphic requiems

scribbled on your tombstone in tones
of gravestone grey.

The sunset plum
buried beneath the daunting abyss
of burnt and blackened horizon.

In darkly winter whispers, you lie waiting.

Behold, the vernal symphony beckons—

its first chirp,
green shoots of snowdrops
and full moon mystique,
mirth and merriment
of patchouli, chrome and clover—

they rouse you to the
tangerines of a sunrise pirouette.

A NEW ME

Topaz and laughter,
citrine fractals in golden flare—

sands of time in prism's ancient hourglass.

Like Perseids' silvered shimmer,
they dribble down from the ebony moleskin
of my past,

unwrapping me in the new breath
of razzmic effervescence.

Lo, I bloom in the charming blurbs
of myrtle crêpes

amidst beryls and garnets
of a banjo's plainsong—

rhapsodies of a new me
awaken in time's rufescent palette.

EMPTY HOME

From the kohl delusions
of the blue, desolate voids,

like a homing bird,

you fly back to our silken nest
of moonstones and bedtime fables

every night,

and lull me to the lilac lilts of your starlit serenades.

But why haven't you come home today?

At the ashen shores, I wait.

Beside the drowning dusk's silent laments,
with empty wingbeats and wails of hazy aches,
I wait.

Heart in sighs of muted greys and sombre shades.

Bruised.

Scattered.

DANCE BEATS

Thrums of orphic drums in choral melody,

gonglike cymbals in sibylline upswell,

amber vignettes
throb in anklets' jingles of sparkly sizzle.

In sways of fluid pirouettes,
you glide on glittery drizzles of irised hums—

blushing tendrils of timeless elegance,
illumined.

On morning's endless anthems
of rose and velvet musk,

you quickstep into a claret trance
of spectral dazzle,

while whiffs of an euphonous symphony
swirl in pinks and dapples of a blazing cloudscape.

FADING FOOTPRINTS

Like ochre runes in arabesque flair,
jewelled amulets trance in hazel glyphs—

myriad grains of our footsteps on earth's
fleeting shoreside.

But, churning in surging torrents,
waves of scarlet rage,

they curl and crest to browbeat them,
throw them into ruins and barrens.

Yet, we tame our frailty,

return in blazing trails of a reborn phoenix
to scribe beryl rhymes of wordless poesy,

afresh,

every time.

DUST TO DUST

An elusive epicedium of mournful balladry—

dust returns to dust
in soft sighs of ghastly corvids.

Cradled in cosmic mystery,
souls unfurl in whorls of canorous ripples.

Like caterpillars
that rise to the bliss of the unbound blue

from the chrysalis of mortality
on the wings of fairy butterflies,

on arcane canticles of new moon nights,
souls waltz to the chords of trumpet refrains

to the radiant lightscape of ether and angelsongs.

SPINNING TOPS, CHASING SHADOWS

Like a spinning top, we spin,
whirl in baffling paradoxes.

Feral twirls,
reckless swings in frenzied pace,
dizzied ecstasy.

In puzzling riddles we spin,

wooed by wild whims and primordial mythos
that lull us numb.

Caught in the vortex of swivelling tailspins,
we vacillate between worlds,
chasing chimeric dreams.

We drift as wandering verses of an eerie dirge,

only to wane in elegiac hues of oblivion
in sobs and in teary adios.

WAITING

Sea moans in aching whines,
crashing in frothy bits.

Bawling waves rumble in greys and haze
of lingering emptiness.

In requiems of dismal whispers,
shorebirds console each other.

Frayed horizon darkens

scattered amidst the cinereous wall art
of broken rainbows and solemn threnody.

My heart too pains.

Why haven't you come back to me

in spring's renascent brushmarks
of crimson gold and plums of purples?

DISILLUSIONMENT

The last wink of the topaz dusklight blurs,
fades in soulful adieus in skyline's shrouds of
charcoal and rusty graffiti.

Doleful breaths of the blue hour—

on shattered notes of ebonied knells,
woeful laments descend on wolfsongs
and whippoorwill wingbeats.

The chokeberry sky weeps.

In lilts of bubbly glee,
moonlit waves visit earth's shores for dainty shells,
folklores and birdcalls,

but return with
vacuous echoes of midnight wails,
forlorn heartbeats.

LIGHT TRAILS

In the orphic symphony lulling in its
opalescent bosom,
light holds a lyrical melody.

At the ebonied abyss of the empty skysill

where sullen mattes sneak in
on the raven elegies of ominous naiads,

clad in glassy luminescence,

it skirrs up as a firebird in ethereal abstracts
of elusive mysteries,

razes sable delusions,
strews ichor in lustrous contrails,

and sings ballads
of birdsongs and morning mist
in streams of sibylline sweeps.

HEART OF THE HURRICANE

Whizzing on dizzying swirls of virulent rage,

its feral fury shrouds me
in frenzied shades of ruin and rot.

Freak and fiery,
hurricane is infernal,

grim and gothic,
harbinger of doom, it's soulless havoc.

Yet, in its windswept twirls
of whirling chaos,

it hums sapphire psalms in cryptic refrains.

In the eye of the storm,
in its sanctuary of lull and stillness,

I bloom in delicate cadence of gold
and dawn-lit rainbows.

ETERNAL YEARNING

Forlorn notes of an elegiac flute,
mournful dirges in woebegone runes.

Bewailing,
in tendrils of sombre sighs,
the lonely fay aches for her lost love—

to caress her in soft-winged wisps
of cicada chorales,

fade in the silver aquarelle
of May moon's muralled splendour,

etch the twilight vermilion on her forehead,
and veil her in festive pastels,

nuptial litanies of lavender dahlias.

FROM THE ASHES

Contrails of streaming embers
in carmine luminance,

horizon ablaze in towering bonfire
of a celestial flambeau.

And lo,
from the smithereens of smouldering ruins,

on feathers of firelight,
lighted fractals of emeralds,

the phoenix rises from the debris of mortality
on zephyr's spirited rhapsody.

Swings of its wings—
gentle sweeps of bloodstone and burnt garnet.

Barcaroles of an oneiric mystery
soar up in crimsons of immortality.

WISTFUL LONGING

Charmed by the ardent calls,
aureate lores of zizzing sands,

draped in the parched dreams
of pebbles and windblown reeds,

the river thirsts for the surging swell
that carries it adown

to the ocean's never-ending hankerings

in jewel-green serenades of willows
and berry bush.

Sunk in the voids of specious ravines,

in soulful blues of weary sighs,
the river weeps—

her scattered hopes
adrift in ripples of ebon and obsidian.

THE CALL OF DIVINITY

Amidst the silver trills of timeless carillons—

incense,

crucifix,

coloured rosary,

sylphic sways of sacred flames,

on weaves of aurulent rhymes,
soft peals of alleluias unfurl.

Like dewy-eyed doves, they waft up
on the wings of ethereal whispers.

The shepherd's flute plays
wistful hymns in woodwind notes.

Twilight leaves canorous streaks
of lilac plainchants,

like ivoried oracles of early dawnlight
that unleash hues of elysian love
in shimmering splendour.

Every cell dapples in iridescence of aery scarlets
to the call of divinity.

MAD ABOUT A MAD, MAD WORLD

Peaks of ecstasy, pits of agony.

Betwixt the two,
it hurtles, plunges us into umbral depths
of bewildering abyss.

Our serenity it teases,

sensibility it razes,

shoves us into the nadir of a dark, chimeric fantasy.

Yet, like drunken shadows that chase emptiness,
we extol it, call it fun,
vie to hop on the carousel of illusions.

Roller coaster—

weird world of mazy twizzles,
eddied world of chaotic frenzy.

VULNERABILITY

Trapped in the eerie labyrinth
of elusive tendrils,

fragile, we struggle.

Feral streaks,
artful lures of spider's pyrite webs.

Like fire ants of bronze and copper whispers,
myriads of scurrying limbs,

vicious as they are.

They hurl us to the vacuous chasms
of endless oblivion.

Mired in the nightmare
of ceaseless cacophony,

caught in the rusty fallacies
of obscure conundrums,

like hapless flies, we struggle.

THE SPRING THAT HASN'T VISITED ME

How many springs
have mesmerised this wintry desolation

painting it tangerine
with its crystal brushstrokes
of blushing chroma!

How many spring flowers
have bedazzled this arid wasteland
with their seraphic hues,

wrapping its barrens
in whorls of gossamer rainbows,
ametrines and scented peonies!

Tell me, why hasn't spring visited me

with its rustling posies of seagrass
and bergamot,

tinged my withered yearnings
with sparkly flashes of ember reds
and amber chirps?

Tell me, why hasn't spring assuaged me,

left its calming lullabies
on my shrivelled heartstrings?

FLUTTERING BALLERINA

A wayward wind
whooshed through the leaves
of a baronial beech,

swung down in a slinky glissade,

wove arabesque strains
in snazzy curlicues through your hair.

Elated, your twilit silhouette
glides into a fluttering ballerina,

your rustled longings
mantled in silver-sequined allegro

twirls to the tender echoes
of a warm, violet viola.

You whirl to unfurl!

SPRINGING HOPE

In the granite skies where dark stars lurk,

sombre requiems grieve
in cinereous cadence.

Forlorn groans in doleful runes,
raven's rhythmless winter cry.

Yet, in the shadows of the grackle black,
in hopeful knots,

I wait—

I wait for the dawning glow of the chalcedony gold.

Amidst the gentle hums
of daisies and dogwood shoots,
siskin's triumphant chorus,

in lace and in velvet,
rainbows bloom in neons and dapples—

luminous aubades of the unveiling spring.